The ABCs of Chanting The Holy Names of God

Krsnanandini Devi Dasi

The ABCs of Chanting the Holy Names of God

Krsnanandini Devi Dasi

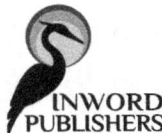

INWORD
PUBLISHERS

For more information please contact:
krsnanandini@gmail.com
www.krsnanandini.com

Cover Artwork: Hari-Gaura Bilal Ziyad
Proof reading and editing: Peter Antonakos
Interior design and layout: Inword Publishers

Inword Publishers:
InwordPublishers.com

Dedicated to His Divine Grace
A. C. Bhaktivedanta
Swami Prabhupada,

Founder-Acharya of the International Society for Krishna Consciousness (ISKCON). He chanted the holy names purely and spread God's holy names, at an elderly age, all over the world with great love, sacrifice, and potency.

The chanting of the holy name is the only means to cross the ocean of nescience. Similarly, the Kali-santarana Upanisad states.....

hare krishna hare krishna
krishna krishna hare hare
hare rama hare rama
rama rama hare hare

"These sixteen names composed of thirty-two syllables are the only means to counteract the evil effects of Kali-yuga."

Table of Contents

INTRODUCTION

I was eighteen or nineteen when I was introduced to the *Bhagavad-gita As It Is*. I didn't know then that this book had been respected and appreciated by thoughtful men and women for thousands of years including Gandhi, Thoreau, Dr. Martin Luther King Jr., Emerson, and George Harrison of Beatles fame. I just knew that reading it underscored my understanding that there is one unlimited God, who cares for each and every one of his creation. In the *Bhagavad-gita*, the Supreme Lord declares that he is the seed-giving father of all of the unlimited living beings in all planets throughout all material and spiritual universes and that we are all, in our essence, not material, but spiritual.

An overwhelming sense of God's love for us came pouring through that book, and I understood that Krishna, or the Supreme God, was ever-present and had already provided a way out of the suffering, ignorance, and pain that plague many of the beings on this earth. I also understood that he wants us to be happy and that happiness is our real nature. That's why we all want a world where we can trust our neighbors, where we care for our families in healthy and loving ways, where the earth is clean and pure again, and where we don't have to be depressed or sick. Given the terrible imbalances in contemporary society, it seems that it's going to take a miracle to make our wholesome desires a reality. That miracle is the holy name of the Lord: *Simple. Profound. Effective.*

In *The ABCs of Chanting the Holy Names of God*, we talk about the benefits and potency of calling upon the name of the Lord, an activity authorized for this age, in every one of the world's major religions. We discuss how sounds can lift us or degrade us, and we emphasize how the holy name of God is the most purifying, attractive, and healing of all sounds. May you find the spiritual strength to take up this simple process of sincerely calling on the name for a beneficial and fulfilling life.

"In the beginning was the word and the word was God and the word was with God."

SOUND VIBRATION

Sounds Change Things

Sounds permeate the atmosphere on all levels. Just recently some scientists (Collective Evolution, September 2, 2011) demonstrated that DNA can be reprogrammed by words and frequencies! Just think about the mind-boggling implications of this discovery. How would we all be impacted when we realize that words or sounds can change forms and shapes at the most fundamental level?

Authors Grazyna Fosar and Franz Bludorf state that the human DNA is a biological internet that is far superior to the artificial one in many aspects. In addition, these authors say there is evidence for a whole new type of medicine in which DNA can be influenced and reprogrammed by words and frequencies without cutting out and replacing single genes. Already, in Russia and other places, scientific research explains phenomena such as clairvoyance, intuition, spontaneous and remote acts of healing, self-healing, affirmation techniques, unusual light and auras around people, the mind's influence on weather patterns, and much, much more.

Based on this research, it is evident that more and more scientists are acknowledging that sound impacts forms, shapes, and even DNA, and they are intrigued by the possibilities associated with such discoveries.

Thoughtful people realize that now more than ever, we need some fundamental transformations in our world. There is just too much mental and physical illness, climate change, famine, alienation, pestilence, war, and many other ills troubling everyone all over the globe. These negative consequences are all reactions to the fact that we (human beings) are not in harmony with natural, divine laws or principles that govern our behavior and earthly processes. *But just as negative sounds have caused us great difficulties, spiritual sounds can also bring about positive growth and peace.*

Confirmation from ancient scriptures:
"Flooding the mind with transcendental sound (of the holy name of the Lord) is just like stepping on the pin of a bomb: All those misconceptions of material suffering and enjoyment are shattered, murdered, and the material mind is conquered wholly, leaving no enemies behind. The mind then reflects the spiritual knowledge, quality and energy of the soul itself. The *maha-mantra* floods the mind with affirmative suggestions of truth. By uttering the pure sound of the *maha-mantra* one invades the very cause of everything that exists. The mind, body, soul, and even nature itself can be changed into transcendental nature by one heart-felt exclamation of 'Hare Krishna!' "—Srila Bhakti Rakshaka Sridhara Maharaja, *The Descent of the Holy Name: A Gaudiya Vaisnava Perspective.*

Sound: The Seed of All Creation

The ancient Vedic scriptures have declared that sound is the seed of all creation. At the beginning of creation, the Supreme Lord said, "Let it be," and it was. Sound vibrations can build and heal, or pollute and destroy. Sounds enliven and inspire or degrade and discourage.

"It is stated also in the Vedanta-sutra that sound is the origin of all objects of material possession and that by sound one can also dissolve this material existence. Anavrittih sabdat means 'liberation by sound.' The entire material manifestation began from sound, and sound can also end material entanglement, if it has a particular potency. The particular sound capable of doing this is the transcendental vibration 'Hare Krishna.' Our entanglement in material affairs has begun from material sound. Now we must purify that sound in spiritual understanding. There is sound in the spiritual world also. If we approach that sound, then our spiritual life begins, and the other requirements for spiritual advancement can be supplied. We have to understand very clearly that sound is the beginning of the creation of all material objects for our sense gratification. Similarly, if sound is purified, our spiritual necessities also are produced from sound." — *Srimad-Bhagavatam*, 3.26.32, purport.

THE SOUND OF GOD'S NAMES

Nature of God's Name

"The holy name is divine and situated in the paramount spiritual realm, it is super-excellent devotional service and the best purifying agent, showering love of God. It is the essence of all scriptures, the cause of everything, the supreme Absolute Truth, the most worshipable object and acts as the supreme spiritual instructor and guide." — Bhaktivinoda Thakura, *Sri Harinama Cintamani*.

"May Krishna's holy name, which is a reservoir of all transcendental happiness, the destruction of Kali-yuga's sins, the most purifying of all purifying things, the saintly person's food as he quickly traverses the path to the spiritual world, the pleasure-garden where the voices of the greatest saints, philosophers, and poets play, the life of the righteous, and the seed of the tree of religion, bring transcendental auspiciousness to you all." — author unknown, *Padyavali*, verse 19.

God's Name is Purifying; the purest sound and form of knowledge

Chanting or vibrating the holy names has immense potency to purify us and heal our troubled planet.

Hare Krishna, Hare Krishna,
Krishna Krishna, Hare Hare
Hare Rama, Hara Rama,
Rama Rama, Hare Hare

In Kali-yuga, if the Vedic maha-mantra is chanted regularly and heard regularly by the devotional process of sravanam kirtanam, it will purify all societies, and thus humanity will be happy both materially and spiritually.

Srimad-Bhagavatam 4.38.14 purport
Srila Prabhupada, Founder-Acharya ISKCON

In this quarrelsome Kali-yuga age characterized by trouble, difficulty, and arguments, the divine sound vibration manifests to purify the atmosphere. Our atmosphere has become polluted — not just by chemicals in the air and water, but by the lies and untruths that people tell and by the profanity, gossip, and negative words that come steady and unrelenting from some people's mouths.

All these negative sounds contaminate the air, "bring down the vibe," and produce

- increasing violence;
- suffering, wars and crimes;
- mental illness; and
- physical pain.

One great saint has said, "Many disease epidemics are the direct result of the injustices, lies, and unfair judgments that often occur in contemporary courtrooms." What can counteract this horrendous attack of negativity through sound? — the holy names of God. They are the topmost sound.

"By the very hearing of his holy name, one is purified." — *Srimad-Bhagavatam*, 9.5.16.

"Even if he be distressed or degraded, any person who chants the holy name of the Lord, having heard it from a bona fide spiritual master, is immediately purified. Even if he chants the Lord's name jokingly or by chance, he and anyone who hears him are freed from all sins." — *Srimad-Bhagavatam*, 6.2.14.

God's Name is Absolute, Non-sectarian

In every bona fide religion, devotees, believers or servants of God, are instructed and reminded that calling upon God's holy names is both powerful and necessary:

"The holy name is a beautiful transcendental touchstone — it is the supreme goal. There is nothing higher than the holy name. I therefore worship the holy name" — *Prayers to Sri Nama*.

"The most beautiful names belong to Allah (God), so call upon him by them." — *The Holy Qur'an*, Surah 7, Ayat 180.

"He that calls upon the name of the Lord shall be saved." — *The Holy Bible*, Romans 10:13; Acts 2:21; Joel 2:32.

"Any nomenclature which is meant for the Supreme Lord is as holy as the others because they are all meant for the Lord. Such holy names are as powerful as the Lord, and there is no bar for anyone in any part of the creation to chant and glorify the Lord by the particular name of the Lord as it is locally understood. They are all auspicious, and one should not distinguish such names of the Lord as material commodities." — *Srimad-Bhagavatam*, 2.1.11.

SOME BENEDICTIONS OF GOD'S NAMES

Since Lord Caitanya, the most merciful Lord, has informed us in his *Siksastakam* prayers that his holy names "alone can render all benedictions." We are sharing below just some of the many specific and unlimited benedictions that come with chanting of the holy names of the Lord:

"O king, constant chanting of the holy name of the Lord after the ways of the great authorities, is the doubtless and fearless way of success for all, including those who are free from all material desires, those who are desirous of all material enjoyment, and also those who are self-satisfied by dint of transcendental knowledge." — *Srimad-Bhagavatam*, 2.1.11.

"There is no other way, there is no other way, there is no other way, other than chanting the holy names of God for peace, prosperity, and well-being in this age." — Vedas

"One who, at the time of death, chants the holy name, 'Krishna! Krishna! Krishna!' will not have to chant any other holy name to be delivered. Among all the names of the Lord, the name Krishna is sufficient for liberation. In fact, [in front of the name of Krishna] other holy names of the Lord feel embarrassed, like an unemployed person who has no work." —Sanatana Gosvami, *Sri Hari-bhakti-vilasa*, 11.502.

10

"Ghosts and evil spirits cannot remain where there is chanting of the holy name." — *Krsna, the Supreme Personality of Godhead.*

"If one offenselessly utters the holy name even imperfectly, one can be freed from all the results of sinful life." — *Sri Caitanya-caritamrta, Antya-lila* 3.61.

God's Name Offers Protection

When I was younger and had been practicing the Vaishnava science of bhakti-yoga (the yoga of reviving our dormant love of God) for a few years, I remember taking a walk on a gorgeous summer morning. It was early — the birds were chirping merrily, very few people were stirring, and the brilliant sun engulfed everything with its warm and friendly rays. Cool breezes gently fanned the earth. My hands were in my *japa* (prayer) bag, and I was chanting the holy names quietly, relishing the beauty and serenity of the moment. Suddenly a huge dog came leaping toward me, barking ferociously. Advancing rapidly, his menacing face was about three feet away. Surprised and feeling utterly helpless, I closed my eyes and screamed, "Krishna!" The barking stopped, I opened my eyes, and the dog had disappeared!

Another time, it was much later in the evening. I was visiting my eldest brother in Detroit. This was in the "ancient times" of the 1980s when there were no cell phones. It was late and I had stayed too long at a park. I was walking quickly back to his place when I noticed steps mimicking mine on the hard pavement. On the apparently deserted street, I glanced back and saw a man (who didn't look very friendly) following me. As I turned the corner, the steps turned with me. I started walking quickly, and the steps picked up their pace too. I was becoming fearful and still had ten minutes or more before I arrived at my brother's apartment building.

My heart started pounding and I began to sing "Hare Krishna, Hare Krishna, Krishna Krishna, Hare Hare, Hare Rama, Hare Rama, Rama Rama, Hare Hare." I increased the volume of my singing, getting louder and louder the faster I walked. I was really praying to the Lord, calling on him desperately. Suddenly, I looked back, and the man was gone! It was as though he had disappeared into thin air! I ran all the way back to my brother's apartment, thanking the Lord for his protection, marveling at the strength and reality of the name.

God's Name Offers Liberation

It is the best of all vows and the highest form of meditation. It gives the ultimate auspicious results and is the most sublime form of renunciation. Chanting the holy names of God is a matchless spiritual activity, the holiest of pious activities, and the supreme path of self-realization. It offers the greatest liberation and goal.

"The holy name of Krishna is the highest benediction, above any other benediction; it is sweeter than the sweetest honey, the eternal fruit of transcendental knowledge of the tree of the entire scriptures. O best of the descendants of Bhrigu, if anyone chants Lord

Krishna's name just once without offense, whether he chants with faith or indifferently, the holy name immediately liberates him." — *Skanda Purana*, Quoted in *Hari-bhakti-vilasa*, 11.234.

"Those names which are part of the transcendental lila of the Lord are considered primary names. Names such as Govinda, Gopala, Rama, Radhanatha Hari reveal the eternal lilas of the Lord, and by chanting them the living entity gets entrance into the spiritual world."

Harinama-cintamani, Bhaktivinoda Thakura

God's Name Offers Love of God

"I do not know how much nectar the two syllables 'Krish-na' have produced. When the holy name of Krishna is chanted, it appears to dance within the mouth. We then desire many, many mouths. When that name enters the holes of the ears, we desire many millions of ears. And when the holy name dances in the courtyard of the heart, it conquers the activities of the mind, and therefore all the senses become inert." — Srila Rupa Gosvami, *Vidagdha-Madhava*, 1.12.

"The Supreme Personality of Godhead is so kind to the conditioned souls that if they call upon him by speaking his holy name, even unintentionally or unwillingly, the Lord is inclined to destroy innumerable sinful reactions in their hearts. Therefore, when a devotee who has taken shelter of the Lord's lotus feet, chants the holy name of Krishna with genuine love, the Supreme Personality of Godhead can never give up the heart of such a devotee. One who has thus captured the Supreme Lord within his heart is to be known as *bhagavat-pradhana*, the most exalted devotee of the Lord" — *Srimad-Bhagavatam*, 11.2.55.

In this Age, the most recommended holy names are the maha-mantra, or Great Chanting for Deliverance:

> *Hare Krishna, Hare Krishna,*
> *Krishna Krishna, Hare Hare,*
> *Hare Rama, Hare Rama,*
> *Rama Rama, Hare Hare.*

Special Benedictions of Sankirtana— Glorious Congregational Chanting of the Holy Names of God

When chanting the holy names of God is done privately or quietly, it is called *japa*. When chanting is done in groups or congregationally, it is called *kirtana* or *sankirtana*. The following verses describe the benedictions of *sankirtana*. The scriptures inform us that those "with sufficient intelligence will worship the Lord in this age by congregational chanting of his holy names."

14

Sri Siksastakam

Text 1

ceto-darpana-marjanam bhava-maha-davagni-nirvapanam
shreyah-kairava-chandrika-vitaranam vidya-vadhu-jivanam
anandambudhi-vardhanam prati-padam purnamritaswadanam
sarvatma-snapanam param vijayate sri-krishna-sankirtanam

Glory to the Sri Krishna *sankirtana*, which cleanses the heart of all the dust accumulated for years and extinguishes the fire of conditional life, of repeated birth and death. This *sankirtana* movement is the prime benediction for humanity at large because it spreads the rays of the benediction moon. It is the life of all transcendental knowledge. It increases the ocean of transcendental bliss, and it enables us to fully taste the nectar for which we are always anxious.

Text 2

namnam akari bahudha nija-sarva-shaktis
tatrarpita niyamitah smarane na kalah
etadrishi tava kripa bhagavan mamapi
durdaivam idrisham ihajani nanuragaha

O my Lord, your holy name alone can render all benedictions to living beings, and thus you have hundreds and millions of names like Krishna and Govinda. In these transcendental names you have invested all your transcendental energies. There are not even hard and fast rules for chanting these names.

O my Lord, out of kindness you enable us to easily approach you by your holy names, but I am so unfortunate that I have no attraction for them.

Text 3

trinad api sunichena
taror api sahishnuna
amanina manadena
kirtaniyah sada harih

One should chant the holy name of the Lord in a humble state of mind, thinking oneself lower than the straw in the street; one should be more tolerant than a tree, devoid of all sense of false prestige and should be ready to offer all respect to others. In such a state of mind one can chant the holy name of the Lord constantly.

Hare Krishna
Hare Krishna
Krishna Krishna
Hare Hare

HARIDASA THAKURA, THE *NAMACHARYA*—
The Great Apostle of the Holy Name

apane acare keha, no kare paracara
pracara karena keha, na karena acara

"Some behave very well but do not preach Krishna consciousness, whereas others preach but do not behave properly."

acara, pracara, namera karah 'dui' karya
tumi–sarva-guru, tumi jagatera arya

"You simultaneously perform both duties in relation to the holy name by your personal behavior and by your preaching. Therefore, you are the spiritual master of the entire world, for you are the most advanced devotee in the world."– *Caitanya-caritamrta, Antya-lila* 4.102 and 4.103

These beautiful words spoken by Sanatana Goswami are in reference to one of the greatest saints of the last five centuries, Haridasa Thakura, the *namacharya*, or great example of chanting the holy names of the Lord.

Born in a Muslim family, Haridasa is honored for his exemplary compassion, honesty, humility, and dedication to chanting the holy names of the Lord. He chanted 300,000 holy names of God daily and was a mentor and friend to all.

Ostracized and persecuted because he chanted Hare Krishna and acknowledged that the one God is known as Krishna, Allah, Yahweh, and millions of other purifying names, Haridasa is the best example of how one becomes elevated and connected to Krishna through chanting his names.

Every day, no matter what the circumstance, this *acharya* chanted sixty-four rounds of the holy names loudly, sixty-four rounds quietly, and sixty-four rounds silently. For his refusal to stop chanting the holy names, he was severely beaten in twenty-one marketplaces—all the while, he kept chanting. Later, it was revealed that the pain of these beatings had been completely absorbed by the Lord.

"Oh, how glorious are they whose tongues are chanting your holy name! Even if born in the families of dog-eaters, such persons are worshipable. Persons who chant the holy name of Your Lordship must have executed all kinds of austerities and fire sacrifices and achieved all the good manners of the Aryans. To be chanting the holy name of Your Lordship, they must have bathed at holy places of pilgrimage, studied the Vedas and fulfilled everything required."

—Srimad-Bhagavatam, 3.33.7

BENEFITS AND BLESSINGS OF THE HOLY NAME:
From A to Z

❖

A

Activates our eternal relationship with Krishna.

Adorns our hearts with beautiful, divine qualities.

Agitates our minds how to spread Krishna consciousness.

Alleviates the sufferings of all living entities.

Ameliorates the degraded, polluted conditions of the environment.

Annihilates the demonic mentality.

Attracts all auspicious things.

Awakens the soul from sleeping on the lap of the witch called maya (illusion).

B

Balances the uneven, unsteady mind and gives stability.

Bathes all souls with spiritual bliss, knowledge, and love.

Beautifies the chanter, the chanter's family, the environment, the world, and the universe.

Bestows the highest level of spiritual attainment.

Blesses the world.

Brings peace and joy.

Burns the reactions of all of our sinful activities.

C

Cleanses the heart of dust that has accumulated for millions of lifetimes.

Connects us with our eternal spiritual family.

Conquers envy, which contains lust, anger, greed, false pride, and so on.

Contains all the potencies of the whole spiritual world.

Cultivates real, pure, everlasting love in our hearts.

D

Divides the material from the spiritual.

Dissolves attachment to the material world.

Drives away ghosts or ghost-like activities.

E

Energizes the mind and body.

Educates the soul with real knowledge of the self.

Empowers us with spiritual potency.

Encourages the self on the progressive path back to the eternal home.

Endows the sincere chanter with the twenty-six primary qualities of a pure soul and all good qualities.

Enlivens the senses with unending joy.

Equalizes every living being and the pure representatives of the Lord, like Srila Prabhupada, Lord Jesus Christ, and Prophet Muhammad, give equal opportunity to everyone to reach the highest goal of life, no matter what race, gender, class, and so on.

Extinguishes the blazing, dangerous fire of material existence.

Extricates us from the clutches of *maya*.

F

Frees the soul from material entanglement.

Fulfills all the divine, scriptural promises.

G

Gives intelligence on how to make progress in spiritual life.

Grants eternal bliss, peace, and happiness.

H

Harmonizes all opposing elements in service to Krishna.

Heals the wounds inflicted by our rough experience with the illusory energy (*maya*).

Humbles the living being so that we won't have to be humiliated, and in this spiritual position, we can serve the Lord without interruption.

I

Illuminates: Godhead is light; nescience is dark.

Ignites the fire of pure, uncontaminated love for God.

Includes all the other Vedic mantras – by chanting the Hare Krishna maha-mantra, one gets the benefit of all of them.

Inspires creativity in service to the Lord.

Is the medicine for our sin-sick selves.

Is the best, most-well-wishing friend of the living being.

J

Joins us with other spiritual beings, both seen and unseen.

K

Keeps us steady in our devotional service and in our

progress back home, back to Godhead.

L

Loves us unconditionally.
Lightens the heavy karmic load we carry by gradually reducing our baggage of sin and sorrow to almost nil.

M

Means Krishna (God), and Krishna means his names.
Motivates and moves us to higher levels of spiritual connection and surrender.

N

Nullifies the effects of all sinful reactions.

O

Obliterates ignorance.
Opens the door to unlimited spiritual bliss.

P

Prepares the devotee for entrance into the spiritual world.
Protects the sincere soul from illusion or "fall down."
Provides for all the needs of the surrendered soul.
Purifies the heart of all material contamination.

Q

Quiets the restless and often raging mind.
Quickens our arrival at the ultimate destination, back home, back to Godhead.

R

Reestablishes real religious principles in our life and in our world.
Rectifies the many sins and offenses we have inevitably made in our conditioned lives.

Releases us from the prison of this material world.

Relieves pain and suffering.

Renders all benedictions.

Rises within one's heart like the powerful sun, immediately dissipating the darkness of ignorance.

Reveals the Lord and his eternal *dhama* (home) and one's eternal constitutional position, or *svarupa* (nature).

Revives our dormant and joyful love for Krishna.

S

Saves the fallen conditioned soul from further entanglement and degradation.

Sanctifies the body and mind as a temple of the Living God.

Separates the "wheat from the tare," the truth from the illusion, the good from the bad, the reality from the lie.

Severs our attachment from the non-eternal material body and other mundane, material things.

Shatters the misconceptions of "I am the body or the mind."

Showers us with the nectarean rain of Krishna *prema* (love of God).

T

Takes away all inauspicious qualities, unwanted or unclean things (*anarthas*).

Trades the temporary, unreliable material body for the eternal, all-blissful spiritual one.

U

Uplifts the human spirit.

Upgrades the gross and subtle material experience to a transcendental one.

Unites varieties of souls in one purpose.

Uncovers the absolute truth hidden by so many layers of illusion.

Uproots the sinful seeds of materialistic desires, which keep us bound to the material world.

V

Vibrates on the higher and highest levels of existence.

W

Washes away our sins and illusions.

Wins the hearts of all living entities.

X

Xs out the fallacies, mistakes, and illusions we've held since time immemorial.

Y

Yields unlimited, unending benefits to the chanter.

Z

Zeroes in on the subtlest of *anarthas* (such as lust, greed, envy, fear, material attachment) to eliminate them over time.

The glories of the holy name are not imagination!

"It is a grievous offense to consider that the above-mentioned glories of chanting the holy names of the Lord are unreal or imagination. The holy name of the Lord is non-different from the all-powerful Lord because he is absolute" — *Padma Purana:* 10 Offenses Against the Holy Names.

A FEW OF GOD'S UNLIMITED HOLY NAMES

❖

Achuyta Infallible Lord who never fails or falls down
Adhokshaja The Lord who is beyond the range of material sense perception
Ajita The unconquerable Lord
Allah The God
Ananda Eternal, ever-expanding bliss
Ananta Unlimited

Balarama Spiritual strength
Bhakta-vatsala The Lord who is very kind to his devotees
Bhuta-bhrit One who gives protection to all living beings

Chaitanya The living force

Damodara The Lord who allows himself to be bound by the love and affection of his devotees
Dinabhandu The friend of the poor
Dinavatsala One who is very compassionate to the poor

Giridhari He who lifted Govardhana hill
Gopinatha The master of the gopis
Govinda The reservoir of all pleasure for the cows, land, and senses

Hari The Lord who takes away all inauspicious qualities and imbues the devotee with all good qualities

Hrishikesha The master of the senses

Ishvara The controller

Jagannatha The master of the universe
Janardana The Lord of all the worlds
Jehovah God, the ever-existing

Kalachandji Beautiful black moon
Keshava Lord with beautiful black hair
Krishna All attractive, irresistible Lord, the original person who attracts everyone in all places at all times.

Lokanatha Master of the universe

Madanamohana The Lord who is the attractor of Cupid himself
Madhava The husband of the goddess of fortune
Madhusudana The killer of the demons
Mukunda The giver of liberation
Muralidhara Flute player
Murari The killer of demons

Narayana The resting place of all living entities
Nrisimha The half-man, half-lion incarnation of the Lord

Olorun Supreme Being (Yoruba)

Partha-Sarathi The Lord who drives Arjuna's chariot
Purushottama The Supreme (topmost), original person
Paramatma The Supersoul in the heart of all be living

beings
Rama The one full of pleasure or bliss
Radhanatha Master of Srimati Radharani

Shyamasundara The beautiful black Lord

Trivikrama The Lord who covered the universe in three steps

Upendra The Lord as dwarf *brahmana*
Urukrama The performer of Herculean activities
Uttamashloka The Lord who is described with topmost, excellent poetic verses

Vamanadeva The Lord who appeared as a dwarf
Varaha The boar incarnation of the Lord
Vasudeva The all-pervading Lord
Vamsidhari The one who carries the flute

Yadava The blessed descendant of Yadu dynasty
Yahweh God—"I am that I am"
Yogeshvara The master of all mystics, one who can do everything

REASONS FOR CHANTING THE HOLY NAME
Shared by People from Around the World

—◦✦◦—

We know the holy name of God is all-powerful and purifying. This method of chanting God's names is the *yuga-dharma*, or the religion for this age. We asked some people why they regularly, steadily and increasingly chant the holy name of God and here is what they said:

- Keeps my heart and mind at peace, an even temperament. — Catie, Columbus, Ohio, USA.
- To have a cushion in Kali-yuga and be at peace . — Tarun, New York, USA
- To spend time with Sri Krishna directly. — Iowa, USA
- To be with my guru, and ultimately Krishna. — Stella, April, Nevada, USA
- To know the truth, the whole absolute truth. — CJ, Ohio, USA
- For happiness and peace in the world. — BG, Chicago, Illinois, USA
- To experience freedom from the bullying of the mind. — Niladri, Bloomington, Indiana, USA
- To beg Their Lordships Sri Sri Radha Gopinath for their eternal service. — Gayatri, Sacramento, California USA
- To fulfill my commitment to my spiritual master, A.C. Bhaktivedanta Swami Srila Prabhupada, to whom I

owe my life.—Laxmimoni Dasi, Alachua, Florida, USA

- To become empowered with love.—Anonymous
- I had a dream a long time ago Srila Prabhupada looked at me with a little smile on his face. He said, "Just chant." Besides that, I love to chant after I finish my sixteen rounds. I chant while I cook, clean, or anything else. Hare Krishna.—Radica, Cleveland, Ohio, USA
- I see demons around me all the time and the only "blessed assurance" to keeping me safe and secure is by calling on "Krishna Krishna Krishna!"—Jarvis, Harrisburg, Pennsylvania, USA
- I chant holy names for many reasons. A main reason I chant is to detach from the material plane. As a result, my inner world expands and eclipses material illusions. Blessings to all!—Kat, Cleveland, Ohio USA
- It's a moment of peace, clarity, and a connection to something greater in a pretty messed up world.—Kaustubha Dasa, Ohio, USA
- So I can be engaged in associating with and thinking about the Supreme Personality of Godhead.—Isopanisad, Akron, Ohio, USA
- To please engage me in their loving service, eternally.—Annapurna, Pittsburgh, PA, USA
- Remedies my anxiety and makes me feel in direct contact with Their Lordships in the here and *now*. Chanting is my hotline to the Lord.—Mike, Louisiana, USA
- For inner peace and connecting with the creator of everything.—Syamasundara, Dallas Texas, USA
- Because the scriptures say so. That it purifies our consciousness. Even though I don't feel the instant

results, this only song that I haven't gotten tired of over the years has definitely worked and I can't imagine what wonders attentive chanting (which comes with practice) can do! — Hladini Gopika Devi Dasi, Toronto, Canada

- To deal with baby mama drama. — Akron, Ohio, USA
- Can't even explain without sounding crazy. It just does something to me. — Marcus, New York, USA
- My name is Caitanya. I chant to clear my mind of non-positive stuff. — Elyria, Ohio, USA
- I chant every day for a half hour with the kids because it was one of our dearly departed mothers last requests, and at the end I dedicate it in her name to Almighty God. — Otis, Cincinnati, Ohio, USA
- I chant because it's my quality time with Krishna. — Christine, India
- Hare Krishna. I chant because chanting is an art. From it I can't depart. — Krsna Kumari, Hillsborough, NC
- I feel less attached to my material circumstances. — Bhaja Govinda, Florida, USA
- To be pure in my actions and thoughts. — Anonymous
- Because the holy name itself is the form of the Lord. No need to have temple or formal worship. Thus chanting eliminates material needs. — Krsnakant Patidar, Bhopal India
- To be reminded of what it truly feels like to be home. — Ganga, Massachusetts, USA.

ABOUT THE AUTHOR

Krsnanandini Devi Dasi is a minister, Certified Family Life Educator (CFLE), wife, biological mother to ten—five sons and five daughters—and spiritual mother to many. As Co-director of the Dasi-Ziyad Family Institute (www.dzfi.org), she, along with her husband, Tariq Saleem Ziyad, has worked with hundreds of individuals and couples, providing them with healthy relationship education; has co-presented scores of relationship, family, and youth character building workshops, magazine articles, curricula, and courses, such as the S.E.L.F. (Singles Evaluating Life and Family) Healthy Relationship course, the Young Pioneer Project, Parenting for the 21st Century, and more.

Mrs. Dasi is a well-known speaker, author and co-author of books—such as *How to Raise Your Children Spiritually; Heart and Soul Connection: A Devotional Guide to Marriage, Service & Love; The Booklet of Eights: A Concise Guide to Spiritual Living; All-In-One Marriage Prep: 75 Experts Share Tips and Wisdom to Help You Get Ready Now;* and *Art of Parenting: Principles & Practices*—and articles about marriage, family, spirituality, parenting, and the practical application of bhakti-yoga principles in our day-to-day lives. (See her websites at www.Krsnanandini.com and www.dzfi.org).

Raised in a Christian family, Krsnanandini has studied Islam, Mormonism, and Hinduism to appreciate the underlying unity in all the world's religions. She was initiated in the ancient Vaishnava spiritual culture in 1972 and has been a practitioner of bhakti-yoga (the yoga of devotion to God) since that time. Mrs. Dasi is dedicated to being an instrument of God's joy, peace, and love. She resides with her husband and children in Cleveland Heights, Ohio.

www.ingramcontent.com/pod-product-compliance
Lightning Source LLC
Chambersburg PA
CBHW030312030426
42337CB00012B/683